I0605397

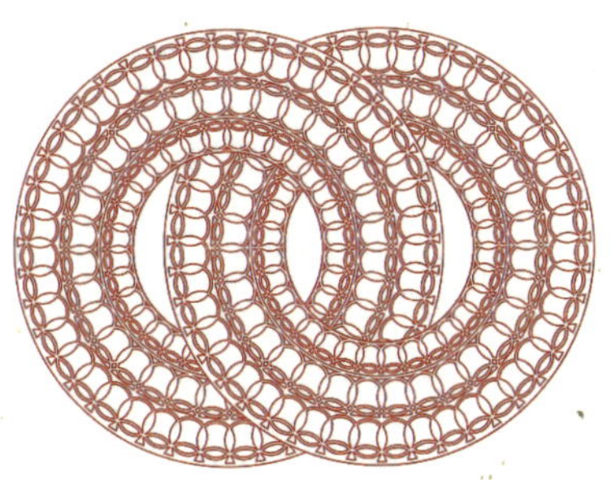

BEYOND THE WATERSHED

Beyond the Watershed

POEMS

Nadia Alexis

CAVANKERRY
PRESS

CavanKerry Press Ltd.
Fort Lee, New Jersey
www.cavankerrypress.org

Publisher's Cataloging-in-Publication Data
provided by Five Rainbows Cataloging Services

Names: Alexis, Nadia, author. | Shockley, Evie, writer of foreword.
Title: Beyond the watershed / Nadia Alexis ; [foreword by] Evie Shockley.
Description: Fort Lee, NJ : CavanKerry Press, 2025.
Identifiers: ISBN 978-1-960327-09-3 (paperback)
Subjects: LCSH: American poetry–African American authors. | Haitian literature. | Vodou–Haiti. | Haiti–Social life and customs. | Abused women–Poetry. | POETRY / American / African American & Black. | POETRY / Caribbean & Latin American. | POETRY / Subjects & Themes / Family. | POETRY / Women Authors.
Classification: LCC PS3601.L49 B49 2025 (print) | LCC PS3601.L49 (ebook) | DDC 811/.6–dc23.

Cover artwork: "Study in Ivy" by Pete de Wint, "New York; the upper bay from lower Manhattan. New York Central System" by Leslie Ragan
Cover and interior text design by Mike Corrao
First Edition 2025, Printed in the United States of America

CavanKerry Press is dedicated to springboarding the careers of previously unpublished, early, and mid-career poets with our Emerging Voices series.

Made possible by funds from the New Jersey State Council on the Arts, a partner agency of the National Endowment for the Arts.

CavanKerry Press is grateful for the generous support it receives from the New Jersey State Council on the Arts, as well as the following funders:

The Academy of American Poets

Community of Literary Magazines and Presses

National Book Foundation

New Jersey Arts and Culture Renewal Fund

New Jersey Economic Development Authority

The Poetry Foundation

For me and my past selves.
For my mother and my sisters.
For those on the path to freedom
and new beginnings.

CONTENTS

Foreword by Evie Shockley xi

Watershed 1
Permission 3
From Haiti to New York 4
Portraits 5
Cassette-Letter '95 6
Ma Ritual 8

Prayer to Èzili Dantò I 11

Trails 12
Daddy Ritual 13
Cantaloupe 16
Definition 18
Lament 19

Prayer to Èzili Dantò II 21

Lessons 22
Browsing the Web While Ma is Dying 23
Granpapa 24
Self-Portrait as a Father's Daughter 26
Hopscotch 27
Scar 28

Prayer to Èzili Dantò III 31

How to Be Friends with a Sex Worker 32
I Don't Own Any Watches 34
Daughterhood 35
Devoured 36

He Reasons 37
Language 39

Prayer to Èzili Dantò IV 41

Thalassophobia 42
How to Make Yourself Small 43
A Horse's Arrival 44
Elegy for the Unborn 45
What Happens When You Hug Your Mother 46
Of Fable & Superstition 48
Prey 50

Prayer to Èzili Dantò V 53

Praise Song for Ma 54
Self-Portrait at the Dominican Hair Salon 55
Aubade After the Storms 56
Dreams of Daddy 58
Suppose You Failed to Cover Your Mouth & So Evil Spirits Flew Out of Your Body 60
Photographing Your Mother 61
Your Therapist Asks in What Ways Are You Like Your Father? 62

Prayer to Èzili Dantò VI 65

Knees 66
Nocturne 67
Cycle 69
Letter to My Friend Robert 70
Someday I'll Love Nadia Alexis 71
Birdwoman 73

Notes 77
Acknowledgments 79

FOREWORD

"Beyond" is a word of great hopefulness. It is often the emissary of imagination, hinting of what can be dreamed and coaxing us to step in its barely believable direction. "Beyond the horizon," whispers to lost souls, praying for signs of familiar territory. Nadia Alexis's *Beyond the Watershed* is a collection of poems that map a too-familiar landscape of violence, while holding faith in a place where a woman like her can see and be her most beautiful self without being punished for it.

A watershed is a topographical term that defines a region where all precipitation—rain, melted snow, and the like—drains into the same body of water. Alexis's collection charts the contours of a conceptual watershed, a region of womanhood—Haitian and Haitian American womanhood, in this case—where the desire for love pours down, but always seems to flow toward men determined to control and contain that outpouring and its sources. Both the poet and her mother are located in this watershed, but Alexis has learned to read the topography. She knows she can't simply keep wishing that their watershed emptied into a different river; she must cross into a different terrain, where her love can run in a new direction, away from a boyfriend who speaks to her body and psyche in the language of bruises, and toward herself.

Alexis brings us with her on a Sisyphean effort to move up and out of the valley of shadows. *Beyond the Watershed* interweaves the stories of her parents, who marry just before immigrating from Haiti to the United States, and those of her own life, her childhood in Harlem, and her young adulthood in Mississippi, reflecting on instances of domestic violence and tracing their impact. The poems all flow into a common aesthetic pool of vivid, intense free verse, via a range of distinct tributaries. Some poems are narrative and direct, offering no respite to the reader and mirroring the experiences of the women described within:

> My chest knows the fire in a man's
>
> palms pushing me against a gate, my skin
> pulled by metal—the fear of running
>
> from a flock of blows, my heart shrinks
> when neighbors learn the sound
>
> of my body whimpered against the wall.

However, Alexis offers relief in the form of the muted music of her lines, their consonance echoing the pressures and pains with explosive imagery. In this way, her poems introduce the inner workings of a woman seeking to survive generational patterns of abuse:

> I was once a wildflower clinging
>
> to hope that the sun could break
> through cinder block doors. I
> remember the names of every man
> who filled my blood with grenades,
>
> redrew the map of my brain, stole
> bread & honey from my kitchen.
> I lay in my own blood & remember
> them enough to write them all dead.

She and her sisters aspire to shapeshifting, through years spent, to borrow a phrase from Robert Hayden, "fearing the chronic angers of" their father's house. Accordingly, yearned-for transformations haunt the collection: "Ma told us about a Black girl / in Harlem who could fly like a bird. We want / to turn into dolphins & fly." Envisioning this possibility, the sisters practice diaspora, inspired by an African American girl's aerial wish even as they transform it for Haitian American girls' oceanic imaginary.

The verbal images of this book are complemented with photographs taken by Alexis. One evocative recurring image, a self-portrait in which the subject is distorted, leads—and follows—us through the collection. Its appearances are tied to the sequence of poems that anchor us in Alexis's journey; each titled "Prayer to Èzili Dantò," they are offered to the Lwa who manifests eros in Haitian Vodou. In the penultimate poem of this sequence, we see the world "beyond the watershed" of intimate partner violence, toward which Alexis is dreaming. The dangers of flooding and drowning, with which she has lived so long, finally give way to water images that nurture and empower her: "In my dreams, I run across the ocean & / become more woman with each wave." In touch with this power and looking through her camera lens, she learns to see another aspect of her mother, who, in this watershed moment, "sits with bells / for eyes, her cheekbones & / life lines rise, adorned sanctuaries." In the words of Ntozake Shange, we might say the poet has started "movin to the end of her own rainbow." *Beyond the Watershed* ends with images resonating with the hope invoked by its title. But, reader, you are not ready to arrive there yet. You are at the beginning of this arc. Enter Alexis's world now, guided by her impassioned poetry, a record of one woman's path toward "becoming my own hero."

Evie Shockley
Jersey City, NJ

Watershed

I arrive at my father's feet a dying
mapou tree. He covers his eyes with
mud while goats feast on my fallen hair.

I hear my mother call for the Lord
to send just enough rain for our lungs
& her carnations to see a new season.

My mother always said boys are best
at taking. I once loved a boy who turned
pomegranates in my yard into salt.

In the mirror, I see a donkey's head without
a home. Daisies dance atop her hair &
she teaches me how to wail for cover.

My mother & I kneel on uncooked rice.
Sweat of our hands no longer remembers
its owner. Our knees become prunes.

One night, I see my father weep & rock
like a forgotten river. How he must know
what it's like to fight against disappearance.

The longer I stay in the home my lover & I
built on this mountain, the more I tire
of circadian leaps into the field of cacti.

Every year Lake Azuéi rises & forces change
on the trees & birds & people of the watershed.
They no longer believe the water will leave.

I spend nights running from hail & company
of vultures. I make peace with the ways
my father & I look away from errors & ruin.

My parents make rituals of warnings & I follow in their footsteps anyway. My mother says I can build a new home from clouds & I believe her.

Permission

shook from temporary asylums
of our beds by crack of leather belt

on back & a basket of screams—
dreamless night & home smelling

of dead herons dad wore on his hands
four volcanoes erupting through our

chests, heavy eyelids tucked under pillows
we ran to the living room leaving fragments

of pink barrettes & hand claps at our heels
wedged ourselves between mom's stolen

strut & graves he planted on her skin
four daughters screamed with scarred

throats & tear-splayed cheeks half-hidden
by her nightgown—assemblage of tiny

fists push against him like gusts of wind
bruises left on the islands of our bodies

we longed for cradled morning
when the sun's mouth was gaping

oh how i secretly wished him to dust
so we would have permission to breathe

From Haiti to New York

The Port-de-Paix sun was hiding
that day. I was on my way to work,
he was standing on his porch, his eyes
trailing me like the wind. His cheeks
stood upright as he bid me *bon jounen*
each morning. I always smiled, bid him
the same & kept walking until one
day he asked *m' ta remen evite'w al mange.*
And this time, I stopped. Told him he
must meet my parents before he could
take me to dinner. Without a second
thought he agreed. That day, I floated
to work like a child. My parents approved
of this man who came to our home with clean,
unfurled hands. Our love was a rooster's song,
sudden as lightning. His heart was made of
mangoes & sugarcane. We married during a year
without a surge, in a Catholic Church whose name
I can't remember. Our parents looked on in wells
of joy, knowing little of the future that would strip us
in the palm of its hands. Cola Lacaye & bouyon
waited for us in the reception hall. We danced into
the signing of the book that sealed the pact we honor,
even when the universe begs us not to, on its knees,
with tears on its back. He flew to New York & built
a home where I joined him, brim-bellied with life. When
I gave birth to a quiet death, I also gave birth to you. Never
marry someone like your father. Whippings from his gravel
tongue leave stains I can't scrub away. His hands rip the soul
from my chest as we struggle to learn English, raise you girls,
and work to keep the rain off our heads. Don't be like me.
I married too soon. There is no love here & the misery
that lives in this home is nothing the good Lord would want.

Portraits

I.
Your little sister sits on your bed & says
she wants to be just like you when she gets older.
The 21-year-old box of you bursts into a butterfly of thanks
& surprise. But the tightness of your stance says
otherwise as you search for words that don't want
your mouth, instead you hand her silence
& ask her about school & trees.

II.
You are standing in black curtains, there are ripe
apples & gold at your feet & they aren't here
to see them. After a lost drive, your family arrives but your
degree is already in hand. You walk downstairs
to greet them & though you feel relief in your blood
& you want to kiss them, you haven't
learned a thing, so you smile & don't.

III.
It's the day after Daddy's birthday & you realize
you forgot. He's walking through the hallway &
you're lying in the dip of your bed editing
a poem. You think of whether or not you should
apologize & say happy birthday.

IV.
Your lover lies in the noise next to you. The side of his
arm lands against yours while your eyes peel away
the flowered wallpaper sticking to the windows. He places
his head on your belly. You hide your smile &
wonder if you should kiss him or tell him a story
of devotion or rub his head. But instead you bring
your hands back to the thunder of your body.

Cassette-Letter '95

Bordered in red & blue, the white envelope sits
on the table until Ma wipes her wet hands on her
flowered skirt & grabs it. I sit on the edge
of the couch & try to hide the black bottoms
of my feet. My fingers dance with loose
thread on my sleeve. *1010 WINS—you*
give us 22 minutes, we give you the world
sounds off in the background. Ma's headscarf
loosens with a deep inhale, her cheekbones rise,
exhale into a smile. Carefully she pulls the cassette
out of the envelope, places it into the oversized
radio & presses play. Grann's voice booms
deep & thick with summer song & long days
on the farm. How she misses us still.
Things are good in Haiti. I try to catch
each word of Kreyol but I stumble
over the ones I can't hold. Savor each
one I can. Grann laughs wide & tells
us next time we visit, she'll have my favorite:
farm fresh chicken, sweet plantains & a bottle
of Kola. Each memory, I taste. The women
washing in the river, the tiny fish racing
around my feet. The man who could only sit
cross-legged all day because of the accident,
my baby cousin grabbing earrings &
whatever he could beyond my arms,
Granpapa & horses he wouldn't let me ride
'cause I was too small. The mountains &
the mountains behind them. For a moment
we're not that far apart & we pretend we know
what year or season we'll hug her again.

The player stops & I ask Ma if we can listen
to Grann once more. The envelope
in her hands is wrung out like a chicken's neck.

Ma Ritual

I watch Daddy stumble
as if his bones split

or the ground
becomes inheritance

too young to carry
him on my back

my hands pearl
with sun   I reach

for his   first man
I was taught to revere

despite the barren language
of him despite there being

no bare path for loving
a father who never learned

tenderness   whose father never
learned   Ma says *somebody*

drenched him
in a curse   but

despite the rot
never to throw away

what's ours   just bury
what's broken in cracked earth

Ma's red hibiscus
fingers rub

Florida Water into Daddy's
bare temples, back, chest

pour wet rag
rain water over his head

return his lungs

Prayer to Èzili Dantò I

He cut my tongue from its home
& left two roosters at war. Rain
betrays earth when it refuses
to join hands. Orphaned stories

still sit in my skin. He cut my tongue
from its home & left me with breath
& pens to etch the truth into water.
I was once a wildflower clinging

to hope that the sun could break
through cinder block doors. I
remember the names of every man
who filled my blood with grenades,

redrew the map of my brain, stole
bread & honey from my kitchen.
I lay in my own blood & remember
them enough to write them all dead.

Trails

When no one is looking I open
my hands & wait for clouds
to spring forth Trails in my palms
sing of thirst I have my father's eyes
& impulse at laughter When morning
is a dark thing I put seeds in a bird
feeder hoping one will come &
give me a reason to return
home Tell me secrets to keeping
a garden alive How many parts water
against unmasking Tell me how to break
down locked windows I have orchids &
weeds & butterflies & sunflowers
& ignoring my father's calls I have gods
in my throat starting a fire

Daddy Ritual

3 a.m. & he paces
the house, spit

collection in his
mouth until he

releases it on
the floor &

opens my door.
I'm sure not

to lift a
limb. He walks

to the bathroom,
turns hot water

on, full blast,
then cold water

all the same,
pulls out hair

pick, pushes it
through his coils

as if to change
their shape or sound.

Emergency
room band on his wrist,

he sits on the living
room couch, starts to

sing his favorite
hymn. I'm still in

bed pretending as he
sings & sings,

rearranges papers &
pillows, turns on

TV & volume as if
to forget

all the shrieks
of the running

water. He will
make sure he's

heard. In the
kitchen he calls

his father's name
& turns on

the faucet. Walks
into his bed-

room, goes back
to sleep. Wash-

cloth covers drain.
House floods.

In morning, we
all step into ruin.

Cantaloupe

I.
I am ten the first time Ma let me split
the skin of a cantaloupe without her.
My knee still bandaged & burning from
a fall I took on the playground that day.
While playing tag, a classmate pushes me
like she wants the ground to remember it.
I don't push back. Tell my teacher instead
& declare I wish it was a half-day. When I
get home, I tell Ma I'm aching for sugar
& numbing. So she hands me a knife & I
lay the tough-skinned fruit on its side.
Cut the two shortest ends & watch them fall
like playing cards. I think back to the breaking.
Stand it upright to make it into a split-sun.
Ma offers to re-dress my wound in ointment.
I dig up & toss innards like they're memories
I want to bury. There is no aloe vera here. Cut
until cantaloupe flesh resembles square-shaped
Lego bricks. Devour several slices before I
place the others to rest in our Tupperware.

II.
My sisters & I climb the plastic-adorned
couch in our living room. Mountains
of clothes & blankets all over the rug
for extra cushion. Today we dive into an ocean—
bellies full of fruit blessings & minds still
on fire from a story Ma told us about a Black girl
in Harlem who could fly like a bird. We want
to turn into dolphins & fly. We know we can wish this.
Feet steadied, hands on each other's shoulders, knees
bent for the journey. There's nothing like the thirst

of Black girls who believe in their own dreams.
Cantaloupe juice can only quench so much. We fly
& dive into the water we built. Bellies pointed up
& down as we lie with bodies transformed into wind.

Definition

Dusk silences the sky as braids unravel
atop me. Tonight I consider burdens
of a shadow. Each section of the hair
is judged by how much it can bend &
make itself beautiful enough to provide
definition. What is a living thing without
some kind of darkness? Each curl strives
to be something memorable & solitary.
Yet willing to make space for growth
of neighbors, even ones that may not
make it past the next leaf-fall.
The more I long to disappear places
of my origin, the more scars follow &
ask to be remembered. As days leave,
so do some definitions. If running toward
light makes a shadow too big, how long can I
make this home of avoidance one of
survival? With risk of becoming a tree bark
of opacity, I add water & oil & consider
how to style these strands I've been given.

Lament

12 years of me pinned to a bed   severed border between

pucker & cheek   he snatched the dove

between my legs   never able to kiss

the next boy   whose lips were as vast   & soft

as home in hands   of grass   waited for him

to pin me down   he never did

I never learned

the next boy loved me   after only 14 days   made me

into a new   bag of dresses   like Ma could only get at tax time

until he left me   for someone new

years later I tried to take breath

from my lungs   love with him meant being

a town   without levees   sinking in floodwater

he broke me down   like food between teeth

surely surely   there was something   better

Prayer to Èzili Dantò II

I lay in my own blood & remember
them enough to write them all dead.
Can I ask you, have you ever gazed
at your lover & found yourself turned

into a time traveler? One day he makes
a mango trail of you instead of bruising
you eternally. Or you are buried alive
in a makeshift grave. Or you are eating each

second of his hands telling you of a kingdom
you never knew. & so the story goes,
we are given powers we never asked for.
Every attempt to leave is a pigeon

sentenced to life as a fledgling. Again
& again, I fall in what I think is home.
People look at me in confusion &
say I must like being held underwater.

Lessons

These days I wonder if he will recognize me
or see how I missed him during our break or how
much I didn't miss the hollow parts. I'm chewing
gum to hide the garlic & nervous in my breath.

I tap my student ID on the card reader, the door's
beep & click usher me into his dorm. Last time I didn't leave
without a black eye & swollen nose to hide.
Skipped dinner & student union meeting that night.

I have a bad habit of forgiveness.

Once in his room, somehow I'm smiling & so is he.
I sit on his bed. My feet touch the hardwood floor. He is on
his iMac doing everything but homework. As we catch up,
he joins me on the bed. I tell him he
shouldn't even try but he hears this differently & now my back
no longer feels air's safety & my legs aren't strong as

I need them to be & he forces & I leave this moment or
attempt to & he ignores my silencing & when he's done he tells
me not to pretend & when I tell him he split me like a pear or that guy
split his cousin, his face opens & he warns me never to call
him a rapist again. Now the lunch & gum I swallowed try
to dislodge their way out of me but the bird in my throat is too big
& he reaches over, kisses my forehead & wipes the wet of my face.

Browsing the Web While Ma is Dying

in the living room & the keyboard
is dough under my ripe fingertips
each time they land as if to drown out
Ma's complaints & sounds of her wooden
knees in surrender to the flooding
of a new week on her feet. The house,
a caged mess & there's food to be made
& no fingers but hers who care to
lift or build & there are eyes that pretend
not to be. She wonders if there will
ever be a day that me or my
sisters will help her, or if we'll just
let her crawl. Mountains grow in my throat,
not big enough to pull me away from this
website or this music or these wallpapered
windows. Ma says God will punish us
with worse children & when she dies
we'll be sorry & I wonder if my sisters
figured out how to love her deeper & why
it feels so hard 'cause she loves us hard
& I wonder if Ma knows about
the night I fell away that umpteenth
time Daddy used his pain to make a
knotted damage of her. I couldn't
understand how she could stay & why
we had to shed our skins each time he
commanded & why our hearts couldn't
just stay in our bodies & why we
couldn't know longer days of walking
in peace & why Ma didn't really
seem to want to be loved no way.

Granpapa

There's a man who lives
in our building in New

York & after you died
I swear he appeared

walking around with
your face. I smile

whenever I see him
hoping he might tell

me something you meant
to say before you left.

If I had another moment
to fly, I would ask you

what's one thing you did
that made you feel

unbreakable? Were the
cassette tapes enough?

Did you ever make art
with what you were

given? Who was the first
person to show you

who you were? What
was Grann wearing

when you met? What
piece of you do you

want us to remember?
In what animal did you

see your reflection?

Self-Portrait as a Father's Daughter

My daddy stands solemn as an elm.
We need juice & toilet paper. He needs
a MetroCard. Today he's a bagger making
rituals of filling plastic with other people's
groceries as he hopes their hands fill his empty
tip cup, although he's a man they don't know.
I'm a tornado & it's summer & the air is a cage
as I pace crowded aisles looking for Kotex &
I consider how fast I can make it from
a different register to the street before any eye
catches how God gave Daddy & I big calves
that push against the wind, how our veiny hands
seem to have touched the earth at the same time.
How many cups does it take to transform
shame? How many hands are needed to bury
aching in a sewer? Daddy & I avoid meeting eyes.
Maybe this helps unflood a home stuck in its own
hurricanes. On my way out the automatic doors,
I pull the loose thread from my dress & think of ways
to kill what seeks to make language of an unrelenting grip.

Hopscotch

safe place for gold
hoop earrings & hair
buns & pink bo-bo's

engine for wins
& losses above
faded white paint

toss a penny
see where it
lands & hop

with the spirit
of dreams &
shoulders free

of the breaking
& the heavy we
never asked for

& it's somebody's
birth month &
soon we will be

on summer vacation
in this park, turning
toward home again

turning the wired
Double Dutch rope
to live longer

loud car music
rivals our hollering
as we hop & hop

across unbent lines
leaves on a ground
we may never forget

Scar

Do you remember that time
he threw you against a fence?

How part of me was snatched
from the right side of your face

like a fish on a hook?

Prayer to Èzili Dantò III

People look at me in confusion &
say I must like being held underwater.
I want to ask them: do those who stay
on hurricane-prone land yearn to sleep

in a home that fails to deliver? Does a quail
long to be remade with a hunter's bullets?
Does the ocean love to be filled with another
man's trash? How many seals have closed

their eyes, imagined all sharks disappeared, &
opened them to a miracle? Do the enslaved not
long to be free? Who among you have begged
for someone to make you feel much bigger

than a fire ant in a room of humans? Who
among you have begged for light to stay
at your doorstep? How many times have you
imagined a lush field of passion vines & keys
to all the doors you wish to escape through?

How to Be Friends with a Sex Worker

I.
Sit in the diner. Wait for her to arrive. Gaze
at the sun in the wall. Pull out your phone. Slide

your thumb across the screen. Look up & smile
when she walks through the door. In two weeks

she is 19. Watch her search through lips & eyes
undone with hunger. Wave your hand. Stand

as she walks to the table. Listen to the screech
of home in the hug you share. Ask her how

she's doing. Sit down. Watch her hair bend in the
August of her fingers. She tells you she's tired but

she's good. She asks you what's new. You tell her
about the latest fight you're having with your man.

She shakes her head & laughs. She tells you about
the Craigslist date she had last night & how her pimp

took all the money. Bread crumbles in your hand.

II.
Jump when you hear the ring. See an unfamiliar number
appear on your screen. Pick up the phone. Try to hide

the worry in your voice. Say hello. Her voice is loaded
with bricks. She says he left her stranded. He took her

purse. No phone. No money. No cigarettes. She is in New
Jersey. She is cold. He is gone. She is crying. You are not

breathing. You close your eyes & curse him again. She
tells you he wants to teach her a lesson. You ask her what

she needs you to do. She says she'll figure it out &
call back. She doesn't. You try to sleep but can't. The sun

rises. You call her phone again. He picks up. You ask him
where she is. He calls you a bitch & tells you to mind

your business. You call him a piece of shit. Promise him he
will pay. Demand to speak her now. He sucks his teeth

& click. You call back. He hits ignore. You call again. He
picks up. He passes her the phone. She says hello. You ask

if she's okay. Your chest is lava. She says she's okay now.
You sigh & tell her there's no home in this life. She

tells you not to worry & that she's really okay.

III.
It's spring break. You meet her at a bar. It's been weeks
since you last spoke. You're late. She looks at you in

annoyance. You laugh & apologize. She tells you she's left
him. You inhale. She works for herself now.

I Don't Own Any Watches

My lover told the air not to come
around here anymore. It doesn't
matter that I wear the pleading
so well. How my chest holds
a sickness only my lover's watch
could have implanted. Saturday
morning & no ray in sight as he
sits in a dorm room chair just big
enough to keep him from falling.
He calls me over. Gives me 10
seconds or he'll teach me an old
lesson. The skin surrounding my
right eye is still died black from
his fist the last time his voice fell
from his lips that way. 10. Lord,
where are your arms? 9. Will today
be the day dead bees fall out of me?
8. The inner winding organs rust
with hunger. 7. How many balled
hands will it take to collapse into
numbers? 6. His foot tap against
the floor sounds like sunken birds.
5. Will I remember what it feels
like to be a woman lodged in an
occasional love? 4. I want to be
soft beyond the orbit of these
veins. 3. I'm ready to bury the
gamble. 2. Who has the recipe
for making a feast with scraps
of time? 1. I sprint to his arctic
lap—can he hear me conjure
wrists disappeared into wildfire?

Daughterhood

Fall leaves sprawled atop the river's
head. The neck of a herring gull
held steady as it carefully faces
the horizon. Some days Ma looks
at me as if I am a yellow cardinal.
Other days, like I am a jammed
door lock resisting its place.
I wish I knew how to sing us
a new season. Hold the skin as if
we have just survived a birthing.
I want to be a better daughter
for both our sake. Whole as hibiscus
& hummingbirds in communion.
Sometimes the clouds speak to me
& tell me to look beyond the burning.

Devoured

My neck knows the curve
of a man's hands, each grain

of strength that lives inside me
mangled. My nose knows the throb

of breath trapped in a pillow pressed
on my face. My belly knows the weight

of a man crushing the empty can
of me. My chest knows the fire in a man's

palms pushing me against a gate, my skin
pulled by metal—the fear of running

from a flock of blows, my heart shrinks
when neighbors learn the sound

of my body whimpered against the wall.

He Reasons

I hate putting my hands
on her   She knows
this   The way I kiss
& rub away impending
swells of her   cheek
after   she makes me
mad   How could she
not know how much
it hurts me   How
I love her more than
I love my knuckles   or
the rivers   I tell
her that all the time
     This is what I'm
sayin'   Women don't
know how to appreciate
a good man when they
have one   Who else
is gonna do all the shit
I do for her?   Give her
more than blood &
bones?   Pain
is temporary   She
knows I won't hit her
again   She know
I'm trying   Sometimes
when I hear her voice
become a wound
I think of how my dad
would come home &
     beat my mother
when I was just a boy

as if   she wasn't
the sky   But
I'm different   I've got
reasons for the lessons
I teach   All
she gotta do
is shut her mouth
sometimes   I'm tired
of her making me
look like the bad guy
& calling me
some kinda
hailstorm   I'm trying
All I want is the best
for her   I grow new
limbs each time I make
her smile   Some days
it feel like all she wake
to do is drive me out
my body   & be
foolish   talk back   & stuff
her ears with bundles
of cloth when I tell her
what to do   as if
I don't have the power
to burn   every crop
she ever grew   split
the moon with my
God-given strength
slaughter
every dove
of its flight
steal her breath
like it was mine

Language

The ocean swallowed a father.
My father's father—whole. His father ate
too many hearts of chicken & women. He ate
his children. My father, one of them.
By the time my mother & father walked
by the same tree, he was born again
into new skins. My father is multilingual.
He knows the cadence of clouds
after murmuration. The language:
algebra equations, American
English, rough hands, Haitian Creole,
turned backs & laughter. He taught me
how to eat the sun & my own tongue.

How to eat the sun & my own tongue,
turned backs & laughter. He taught me
English, rough hands, Haitian Creole,
Algebra equations, American
after murmuration. The language:
he knows the cadence of clouds
into new skins. My father is multilingual.
By the same tree, he was born again
by the time my mother & father met
his children. My father, one of them.
Too many hearts of chicken & women. He ate
my father's father—whole. His father ate
the ocean & swallowed a father.

Prayer to Èzili Dantò IV

How many times have you imagined a lush field
of passion vines & keys to all doors you wish
to escape through? Sometimes I wonder how
I got here & then I remember there's no choice

in how the wounding is served. Daddy always
loved Ma the best or worst ways he knew how.
Ma stayed. When I asked why, answers did little
to fill multiplying craters in my hands. I arrive

at the same cliff she dangled past selves &
dreams from. I wear the same dress & choker.
I use broken nails to draw a tree in the dirt
filled with goddesses who balance buckets

of secrets & jewels on their heads. Never spilling.
I pick up each twig, each leaf, each rock & eat
them all. In my dreams, I run across the ocean
& become more woman with each wave.

Thalassophobia

It's raining again & I want to believe
the sea is a gift & not just a place people
go to die but a home with a floor you can
dance on. They say one way to get over
a fear is to walk toward it despite the bone's
bursting. He is rambling a story with no feet
but I never cheated even when he did.
He plunges my body beneath waves & laughs
as if he hadn't laughed since the last time
he used water to make the skin a wound. Is this
what it means when he says he hates women
but loves me? I try pretending I am a stonefish
or ship or hurricane. He releases me from his
ruined hands & the first thing I see is unfamiliar skies
above a quilt of lost sea gulls. In a stumbling blink
& grasp for water & sun. I know I am still here.

How to Make Yourself Small

Lie in the bed next to him. Pretend
your lover's snoring makes you calm.
Rub your belly & try to press the cramps
away. Squeeze your thighs together
to stop the flow. Fail. Pepper his
sheets with blood. Fold your body
into a mound of fresh laundry. Get up
& toss the sweetened pad into the trash.
Replace it with a virgin one. When he
wakes & roars because he sees a border
of blood between you, try to paint
your body into the nearest wall. Forget
how to shapeshift. Don't ignore him
when he calls you over. Notice how
he refuses to hide his cracked face. Begin
cleaning up your blessing. Remember
what you've learned. No time for gazing
at the blood moon or wishing yourself
into another time. Grab dishwashing liquid
& water like Google told you. Resist
getting lost in a firebrick landscape of his
turned back. Erase yourself as fast as you can.

A Horse's Arrival

after A Horse at the Cardo Beach, *by Valda Nogueira*

Clouds move quickly above your
gait & my feet lodged in glassy,
tainted sand. Your faint-colored
skin hangs, seeming to have aged
quicker than God or your mother
intended. I like to think we arrive
in the paths of each other's hungers.
    Oh mare, I want to ask how
you walk smoothly despite devastation.
Sometimes I can do this too & yes,
I notice how the ocean water turned
on all its fish. How the oysters have
disappeared the more humans force
metal pollution. I ask for permission
to touch your neck & take your lean
forward as a yes. Rest my palm there,
startled. It feels like pulses of three
dancing women in your flesh, perhaps
from another land. When I was a little
girl I thought anything was possible,
like leaving earth on a cardboard
spaceship or becoming my own hero.
    Dear mare, closer now. I know
what it's like to be dominated against
your will. I know what it's like to stand
in the face of other beings' selfishness.
I know I can be selfish. Your black hair,
dull silk blowing in the wind. I search
for answers in your body's shadows
only to stumble, empty-handed &
back into my own longings.

Elegy for the Unborn

You were conceived in the season
of water bearers & wind-cracked lips,

just like your dad. The sky was heavy
as gods between our skin. You were

his last attempt at keeping me
bloodied & jailed but nothing could rip

me away from my free—not even
the test that flew tremors through my

hands. Twelve weeks of you unfolded
in my womb—the unwanted promise

he'd never knew he buried into me. I stood
in a room lined with women & blue-chairs.

The receptionist took my name
like a cashier—told me sit until

the doctor bid me to the back room.
When she finished, I woke pink-

gowned & bare, a sea of guilt
& a casket of relief.

What Happens When You Hug Your Mother

& can't remember the last time
you stepped into shadows of each
other's embrace? This time you're at
an airport many bodies away from
Harlem & her flight is to Miami
where your uncle awaits her aged
unburdened breathing, face lined
with New York's draining, skin
made of cane & river. No earrings
or makeup or attention to her
weathered knees—she's dressed
in an emerald dress so rich, you
can see its song beneath her dark
eyes & you notice the assembly of
pigeons flying toward the ceiling as
though feasts are falling & Ma's
luggage is checked & the air folds
just before parting & you remember
the faint odor of unliving flesh in
your best friend's car after his Mama
died at home & left her things & all
you could do was be a tree for him
& a stumbling smile on your Ma's
face brings you back & your body
drifts into hers & it's not a long hug
or one that speaks of the cheekbones
you share or one that your palms
remember & you leave wondering
if being held by your mother was
supposed to be different, if it was
supposed to be a slow moving

creek or if you was supposed to feel
like last time, whenever that was, you
could feel orchid gardens swollen in
your chest or maybe Ma's lips visited
your cheek & the hug wasn't so brief
& maybe you weren't just her child
but a bruise & you wonder if Ma is
a simmering spring of wonder.

Of Fable & Superstition

Don't step over someone's outstretched
legs or they won't grow. Grow like
sunflowers in a field of other sunflowers.
Grow like skin grows back when it bursts.
Bursting balloons grow with faith & lungs.
The lungs hold what we can't see. See
the fledgling open its eyes & make cake
of flight. Move like the clouds move
with anticipation & the gaze upturned
eyes. Turn your gaze upward & resist
scratching your arm when you are pregnant
& in the middle of a meal. You'll be marked
forever. Blood marks a spot where he left
you on your belly with dirt on your hands.
Place your hands over your broken teeth.
The elders always find some use for
helping another child or three.

Prey

My lover once said a woman is best
with a mouth as a closed door.
If she should want to open it,
let it be brief & of bright blooms.

If she should dare to make herself
bigger than a man with her voice full
of restless bells, she must be ready
to make war with hands bare.

If she can't, she must nail her tongue
to a tree's bark or he'll bury her
into earth's belly. I no longer wish to be
the ground carrying him. No longer wish

to follow rules that drain me of freshwater.
Today I am guilty of becoming a falcon,
every bit of him for my consumption.
For years I have felt alone & dry-bellied,

but tonight I am Èzili Dantò's child
armed with scarred vines & silver.
I strike & he falls like leaves under the
weight of a half-woman, half-mountain.

Prayer to Èzili Dantò V

In my dreams, I run across the ocean &
become more woman with each wave.
Something like you. I fly bruiseless &
renewed by the blue suns. Assemblies

of mothers & daughters sing & laugh
big until we all fly hand-in-hand. We sweat
& become our own guava horizons. Every
coconut tree is a city that welcomes us.

No one tries to take the moon from our teeth.
In this world, we don't have to lower our
heads or bend. Everywhere we go, so does
the water. Our hair shimmies at the clouds

& make songs with the wind. No rape,
no black eyes, no pockets or souls sucked
dry, no one to lead us away from this home.
Everything we can dream is blooming & true.

Praise Song for Ma

Praise the silence. It never leaves us
without our shadows. Praise bees
that remind me I still have breath
in my body. Praise the will in you
despite the weight of him & the world.
Praise the warped toolbox & mirrors
you put in my hands. Praise laughter
after floods try to take everything but
our memories. Praise the skin. It mends
& persists like trees through winter. Praise
the secrets we hold & bare. Praise hunger.
Praise boats we build for escaping. Praise
rain that chips away at walls between us.
Praise how you love to watch birds fly.

Self-Portrait at the Dominican Hair Salon

Somewhere between snowfall
& cherry blossoms, I take
a selfie in hair rollers before
the blowout. Today I am wearing
mustard yellow. My brown skin
glows as if sun rays spring
from the salon mirror to say,
here, take all this good light
& just forget the bruising.

Sitting in Johnny's chair, I see
a reflection of a crowd of pigeons
outside the storefront fighting over
fallen bread. The air conditioner hums
through each hair part like they're cups
of tea that need cooling. I think I hear
someone say *you deserve comfort.* One
by one, Johnny picks pink & purple
rollers from my relaxed hair. Tells me
what healthy looks like & how I measure.

The red & black blow dryer wails
at my scalp, some kind of litany
bidding me to ignore what burns
& the yearn for life without scars or
debris. Dream up a world where a lost
woman can wake up & make herself
a different creature & in the end see
how the hair falls like water spilled with
intention. Praise the gods for every jewel.

Aubade After the Storms

Wounded rooster sings of morning
like it wants to forget the night,

invites my eyes to open like curtains.
Sunlight breaks the windowpane,

reminder that my favorite season is still
here. Mouth of the beach awaits me.

I wake & try to wash what he left of me
in ruins. Towel-press droplets into my skin

like gauze after a drawing of blood.
Grab a blue dress from its hanger

& search for peace in the cotton folds.
I walk down an empty road & glance

at a man's beard, the color of a pigeon's
back. He smiles at me like I am kin.

I smile back though we look nothing alike.
Wind propels my cypress legs forward,

embraces knees that want nothing more
than to pummel the ground. I arrive

at the beach where armies of waves
cut into sand like Ma split fresh bread.

Hairs on my arms stand in longing
for home in my former lover's arms,

despite beating winds of his voice & hands.
They say missing an abuser is normal.

Yet one day you'll return to your reflection
with sky of you more often blue than barren.

Dreams of Daddy

I used to dream my daddy
as the first builder

I knew. His hands thick &
brown & vulnerable as a tree's

bark. Air in the home always
sitting with his light. We

knew nothing of being
water trapped in edges

of glass. His daughters,
ripest mangos picked & built

from his & Ma's skies.
In my dreams I knew

what it felt like to be
in his embrace. Arms

like the tide visiting shores
& seashells & trails in palms—

offerings of water's memory
& sustenance. Always

returning. His laughter
filled with song of jubilant

hummingbirds. He could
take us by our shoulders

quickly, quickly over
frigid, polluted waters.

Build us a new pond. Repair
the nest if ever it should crumble.

He would make sure we knew
we were of the wind & deserving.

Suppose You Failed to Cover Your Mouth & So Evil Spirits Flew Out of Your Body

& your throat became an abandoned
rose garden beneath the blue storm
of your mouth & one spirit is the man
who killed your mother under a wolf
moon, in the middle of the tenth
blackout of the summer & he struck
her with enough help from serpents
& zombies hiding in New York City
alleys after long days of searching
for sugar & freedom, or maybe
there was a spirit of the woman
who flew through the night's sky
with wings made of her sleeping
brethren's dreams & pieces of the
river with her, building a new shed
on mullets & pebbles & mountain
song & blood of women washing
their best, or maybe there are spirits
who are sisters who traded bird & sun-
loved skin & laughter & candy air,
who tended to each other's bruised
backs & ruptured tongues with mango
innards & maybe in the midst of this
you forget to use your palms & forearms
to shield yourself from a voracious fall.

Photographing Your Mother

She's in a blue sequin gown,
blood-red heels & headwrap
colored kaleidoscope.
She is birthsong, her own
city, generous mountain.
When you press the shutter
your eyes are no longer yours.
You are ocean & every speckle
in you weeps. Each selfless gesture
of her is on display. You press
the shutter, only gift you know how
to give. It doesn't matter
that everything tried to get
in the way. Here she sits with bells
for eyes, her cheekbones &
life lines rise, adorned sanctuaries.
This time—one of a few
when you've not failed
as her daughter. Smeared, forgotten
sins. Both your feathers new.

Your Therapist Asks in What Ways Are You Like Your Father?

& you can't recall the last time someone asked you to paint
what you remember of your face in the water.

You remember your father once told you to look beyond the edge
of 133rd & Amsterdam to make your own mountain water,

become a doctor or the good kind of lawyer & don't you forget how
he'd take you to the park as a girl to be renewed by sprinkler water,

your thick coils always frizzed up like the edges of oak tree leaves.
You swallow the seahorse in your throat & remember how sounds of running water

cutting into sinks of the Harlem apartment were hands rubbing his restless
back & how one day you discovered love was the sound of ocean water

diving into earth. Despite its plastic pollution Yemaya still lived
there, didn't she? You remember how your father loved walking into flood water

creeping onto floors as your family slept. How late night bathroom runs meant your feet
winced every time & you wished you could summon the healing of holy water.

You think of how this question makes you feel like someone
is asking you to open every window & door despite you wanting to hide wastewater

that won't seem to leave. You remember how your father spoke of how hands
full of dreams brought him & your mother to the other side of the water

alive. You remember how you are slow to hugging & you can't remember
what it feels like to be held by your father & you think of how water-

sheds have purpose. Nadia, sometimes you stand at the sink too long,
watching the sunlight make sequins of the water cupping your hands.

Prayer to Èzili Dantò VI

Everything we can dream is blooming
& true. I run across the ocean & make it
to the shore. I become a container

of roadkill. I run & run & run & yet
I can't escape the stench of memory.
I blink & I am back under his boot—

see how rubber becomes a flame?
I blink & I am dropped into a film
reel of he & I as contortionists.

My god, it's true how a body refuses
to let go. Every open window & door
leads me back to a crumbling. I am

an expert at clinging to earth until
every hidden battle begins again.

Knees

Lord, give Ma my knees
& maybe she will run
from her husband & his
eating away at her flesh.
No matter the season or
holy day. Give the knees
voice to remind her
of the worth she stuffed
in the folds of forgotten
favorite dresses. Tell her
she must not die in a festival
of red could-have-beens. If
I could leave my boyfriend,
she could leave Daddy, too.
Tell her she can be a new
kind of ocean. Remind her
that shedding is natural,
even after thirty years
married. Some things
just need to burn.

Nocturne

I'm getting used to undressing
    in this dying wilderness. Now that

he's banned from my home,
    when sky darkens & thickens with breaths

that once were, I think I hear him
    outside my front door. This is normal.

Intense fears after the scorching.
    Dormant memories fly out the body's

openings. No warning. Desires
    to avoid places that remind me. Even

if place is home. Tonight a stray
    cat stands on my back deck & wails

as if she's tired of aching for us both.
    My ivory slip hugs me like it knows

it's my own kind of moon. I flip on
    the deck's light. Her amber eyes claw mine

& she runs. Perhaps she doesn't
    want to see me standing like a tree stripped

of its leaves & water.
    This protection order guides me through

split existence—a forest after partial
    clearing. With blinds open, I let the slip become

its own rainfall. Trust the air
    on my uncovered body. Some nights I wish

to rush growth by plunging
    my feet in soil. That I could make sense

of wondering if he's eaten,
    if he mourns. Yet my body can't forget being cut

through its heartwood. Each day,
    I show up everywhere fighting to be a steady dwelling.

Cycle

Song: three cedar waxwings sprawled
fruit drunk & lifeless on concrete.

I clutch my belly still panicked
from overindulgence in salt & sugar.

A couple walks by my standstill
as I consider asking about proper

burials. Yet I arrive at my knees.
My eyes search for a modicum

of berry or breath as I extend a finger
toward a body & pull away. What is

lost is not always meant to be brought
back. I consider the risk of ridicule

in an attempt to be power. Remnant
of kale on my tongue announces itself

& undergirds my thoughts on shapes
of mourning & pleasure. Knees crack

as I rise & wipe sweaty fingers
on your yellow dress. A tincture

to consider whether death is best
experienced by pain or euphoria.

Letter to My Friend Robert

This morning I wanted to write so I changed into my outside clothes
unlocked the door & walked onto my block where I thought of my father
whose favorite hobby is walking up & down & around the streets
of Harlem against my understanding until today when I find myself
seeking some kind of fire in the air & now I'm a couple of blocks
& beats of birdsong away from my Mississippi doorstep passing by
a fenced-in white dog who barks & growls at me like she believes
I've taken something or she is displeased with unshuttered windows
absent of human bodies peering through to see about her & oh
how green it is today that I am almost in disbelief at how
nature changes in a matter of hours or the two weeks it's been
since I returned to the mouth of this trail on a chilly overcast
afternoon I was met with downed trees strewn about as if
all that mattered was their continued proximity to home & this
comforted me despite my deepest love being them standing alive
& today I'm convinced some god came by & dropped off a new
forest & new eyes for those who beg for relief as sudden as this vision
I have of an imaginary father addicted to walking because it lets him
time travel to other worlds almost like watching a film & some days
he doesn't know what he'll get & maybe there's magic in not knowing
that one day you could arrive at the heart of a lake & there are guitars
& drums & keyboards floating in the breeze playing tunes that feel
familiar & unfamiliar & you can dance & pray to the edge of a fallen
leaf turn yourself inside out & oh Robert this trail is a whisperer &
a mirror I wish you could see & please do tell if you have a spot in Brooklyn
like this trail that implores me to take what I need & leave an offering
if I have one to give & journey back to myself to arrive at a blank page
& call it green call it mockingbird call it train call it break call it bloom

Someday I'll Love Nadia Alexis

After Frank O'Hara; After Roger Reeves; After Ocean Vuong

I know this. But again, we offer our wings
for the plucking. Because venturing

into fire some nights, is more
home than dancing on moonlit

ground to worship the reach
& freedom of our shadows.

Untouchable—

this is what we long for.
This is what we know.

It's okay that we make feasts
of memories that refuse to leave

our body. Still. More woman,
than wound. More festival,

than forsaken. Nadia, do not
forget that you are still here.

Here, we are made of tulips
& singing sunsets & tide ever returning

to the doors of new homes we dream up
from thick air. Look how we wear glory

& stumble & jewels we collect
with imperfect intention in baskets

we've found along the way.
A white candle burns for our future.

It matters that we almost killed
our oceans, that we almost let him bury us, too.

Sometimes failures are blessings.
Every moment we spend putting water

& air back into our body is worth
getting to the someday we know is waiting.

Even as we work to shake the fear
of extended hands attached to harmless faces

that remind us of his smothering, of nightmares
of being lost in foreign woods that reject the sun

& us, we will not let scars be the only
map we see. Consider our mother, the hope

in her passed along to us is field of trees
that can't be cut no matter the weapons.

Consider our grandmother & hers & hers.
All of us, daughters of light & steel,

of rivers flowing two ways,
of yearly independence soup.

We've got machete & spirit & our own
everlasting overgrown gardens.

Birdwoman

The pigeon walks to the edge
of earth's shoulder. Wind pries
open its beak, pulls a song from
its maroon throat, wicks the rain

from its wings. I lie in the grass
& pray that one day a man will
protect me from the sleet & earth's
opening. Unlike the others, he

won't make me into crushed garlic
in a mortar. He will see me as the
woman with the vision of an owl.
Woman no longer endangered.

I have just learned how to drive
like roads are mine. An oak tree's
branch bends, makes way for me
to sing. Daughter of this air & hands.

Notes

Valda Nogueria, *A Horse at Cardo Beach*, Photography, 2012, Sepetiba, Rio de Janerio, In Valda Nogueria Porto.

The poem "Someday I'll Love Nadia Alexis" was inspired by the following:

Richard Osler, "Poems by Frank O'Hara and Roger Reeves and Another Poem by Ocean Vuong, Plus a Generative Writing Adventure for Anyone Who Wants To Try It," *Recovering Words*, posted November 20, 2022.

ACKNOWLEDGMENTS

I am grateful to the editors of the publications that published the poems and photographs in this collection, including earlier versions.

Poetry

The American Poetry Journal: "Trails"
Argos Books Poetry Calendar: "Cassette-Letter '95"
Indiana Review: "Suppose You Failed to Cover Your Mouth & So Evil Spirits Flew Out of Your Body"
Kweli Journal: "How to Make Yourself Small," "Permission"
MQR Mixtape: "A Horse's Arrival," "Nocturne," "Watershed"
Mud Season Review: "Aubade After the Storms," "Knees," "Lament," "Language," "Thunder"
Shenandoah: "Cantaloupe," "Letter to My Friend Robert"
Texas Review: "From Haiti to New York"
Tinderbox Poetry Journal: "How to Be Friends with a Sex Worker," "I Don't Own Any Watches"
Visceral Brooklyn: "Daddy Ritual"
Wild Gods: The Ecstatic in Contemporary Poetry and Lyric Prose: "Aubade After the Storm," "Lament," "Language"
Wild Imperfections: An Anthology of Womanist Poems: "Cantaloupe," "Prayer to Ezili Danto V," "Watershed"

Photography

Forgotten Lands, Volume 3, "In Defense of Paradise": "Woman in White, No. 5"
The Southern Register, Winter 2022: "Woman in Dark Pattern, No. 1"
What Endures series, MQR Mixtape, Issue 1: "Woman in White, No. 2," "Woman in White, No. 5"

Many thanks to Gabriel Cleveland and the CavanKerry Press team for giving *Beyond the Watershed* a beautiful home. Thank you, Baron Wormser, Bridget Reaume, and Joy Arbor for your thoughtful editorial eyes. Thank you, Mike Corrao, for this wonderful book design.

Deep gratitude to Evie Shockley for your insightful foreword that beautifully frames the collection, and to you, Eugenia Leigh, Khadijah Queen, and Mahogany L. Browne, for your generous and affirming words about this work.

Thank you to all of my poetry, writing, and photography teachers and mentors along the way, especially Derrick Harriell, Aimee Nezhukumatathil, Kiese Laymon, Melissa Ginsburg, Bisi Ideraabdullah, Vievee Francis, Gregory Pardlo, Rachel Eliza Griffiths, Brooke C. White, and Carrie Mae Weems, among others.

Thank you to Kelsi Long for helping me polish this manuscript for submission, and insisting that the book was ready to be out in the world.

Thank you to those who encouraged me in my youth, especially my childhood friend's father Joseph Kelly, my fifth-grade teacher Ms. Gavin, and my high school English teacher Mr. McDermott.

Thank you to my dope friends and classmates at the University of Mississippi, especially Sadia Hassan, Naza Okoli, Tyriek White, Julian Randall, Joshua Nguyen, Michelle Lynn Ayers, Amy Lam, and Sarah Sgro.

Thank you to my friends Melanie Gonzalez, Patricia Philippe, Nia Jones, Linda Tigani, Chris Kelly, LaMont OyeWale' Badru, Jennie Frost, Ida Harris, and others. I love you all.

Many thanks to the countless people and organizations who helped me get here, and who have cheered me on from NYC to Mississippi, and beyond, especially the Women Writers in Bloom Poetry Salon and Brooklyn Poets, among others. I am forever grateful.

Thank you to my ancestors, who have walked with me all these years.

With love, respect, and thanks to my family.

And thank you, too, dear reader.

CavanKerry's Mission

A not-for-profit literary press serving art and community, CavanKerry is committed to expanding the reach of poetry and other fine literature to a general readership by publishing works that explore the emotional and psychological landscapes of everyday life, and to bringing that art to the underserved where they live, work, and receive services.

Other Books in the Emerging Voices Series

In Inheritance of Drowning, Dorsía Smith Silva
Seraphim, Angelique Zobitz
When Did We Stop Being Cute?, Martin Wiley
Boy, Tracy Youngblom
In the River of Songs, Susan Jackson
Mausoleum of Flowers, Daniel B. Summerhill
A Half-Life, David S. Cho
Uncertain Acrobats, Rebecca Hart Olander
Her Kind, Cindy Veach
Deke Dangle Dive, Gibson Fay-LeBlanc
Pelted by Flowers, Kali Lightfoot
Rise Wildly, Tina Kelley
Set in Stone, Kevin Carey
Scraping Away, Fred Shaw
Rewilding, January Gill O'Neil
My Oceanography, Harriet Levin
See the Wolf, Sarah Sousa
Gloved Against Blood, Cindy Veach
Threshold, Joseph O. Legaspi
Jesus Was a Homeboy, Kevin Carey
Eating Moors and Christians, Sandra M. Castillo
Esther, Pam Bernard
Love's Labors, Brent Newsom
Places I Was Dreaming, Loren Graham
Misery Islands, January Gill O'Neil
Spooky Action at a Distance, Howard Levy
door of thin skins, Shira Dentz
Where the Dead Are, Wanda S. Praisner
Darkening the Grass, Michael Miller
The One Fifteen to Penn Station, Kevin Carey
My Painted Warriors, Peggy Penn
Neighborhood Register, Marcus Jackson

Night Sessions, David S. Cho
Underlife, January Gill O'Neil
The Second Night of the Spirit, Bhisham Bherwani
The Red Canoe: Love In Its Making, Joan Cusack Handler
WE AREN'T WHO WE ARE *and this world isn't either*, Christine Korfhage
Imago, Joseph O. Legaspi
Through a Gate of Trees, Susan Jackson
Against Which, Ross Gay
The Silence of Men, Richard Jeffrey Newman
The Disheveled Bed, Andrea Carter Brown
The Fork Without Hunger, Laurie Lamon
The Singers I Prefer, Christian Barter
Momentum, Catherine Doty
An Imperfect Lover, Georgianna Orsini
Soft Box, Celia Bland
Rattle, Eloise Bruce
Eyelevel: Fifty Histories, Christopher Matthews
GlOrious, Joan Cusack Handler
The Palace of Ashes, Sherry Fairchok
Silk Elegy, Sondra Gash
So Close, Peggy Penn
Kazimierz Square, Karen Chase
A Day This Lit, Howard Levy

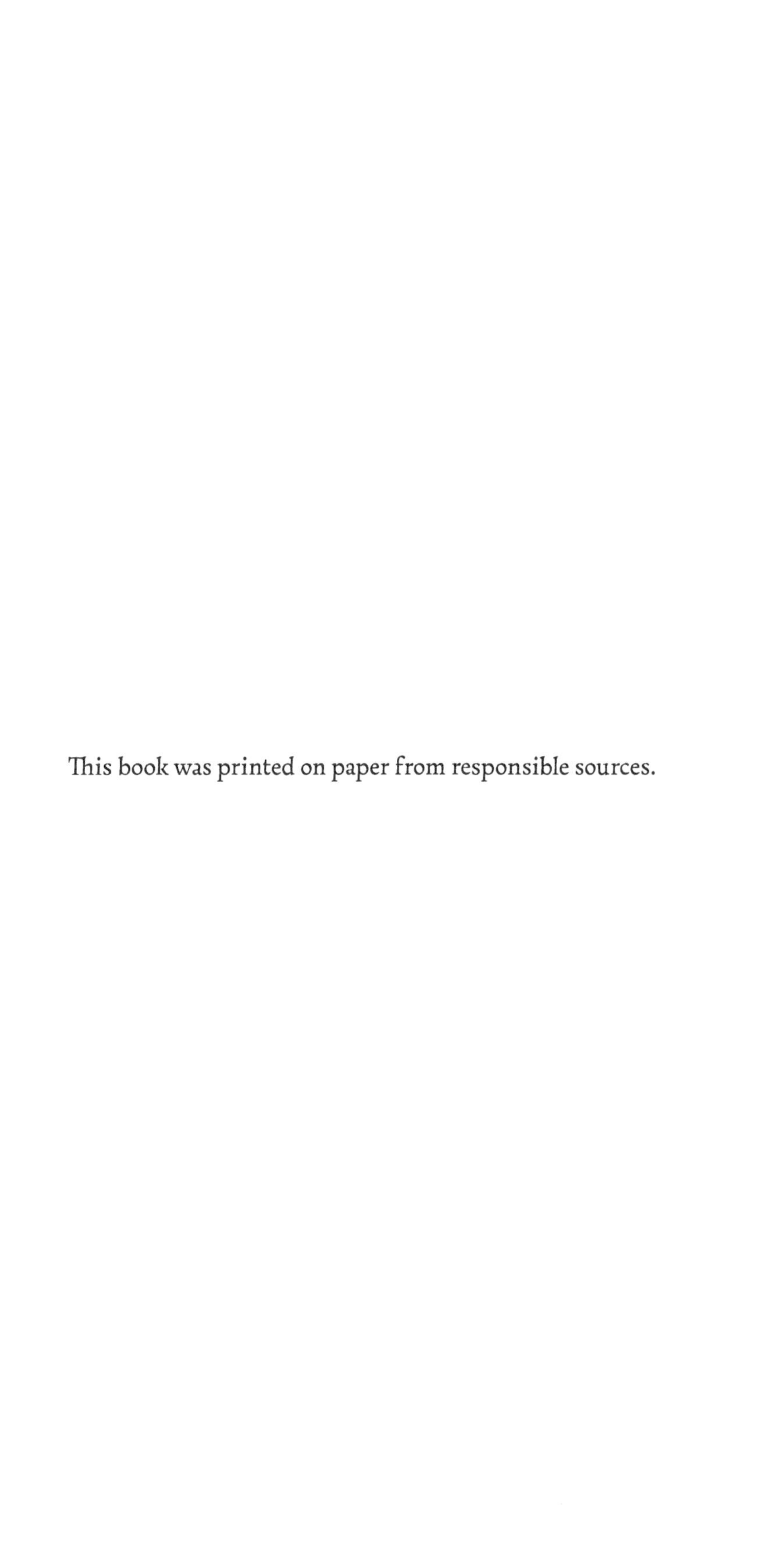

This book was printed on paper from responsible sources.

Beyond the Watershed was typeset in Essay Text,
which was created in 2014 by Stefan Ellmer. Its design
presents historical principles through a contemporary lens.